VAN GOGH PAINTS THE NIGHT SKY

Vincent Can't Sleep

by BARB ROSENSTOCK

illustrated by MARY GRANDPRÉ

ALFRED A. KNOPF

NEW YORK

Vincent can't sleep . . .

so while the sturdy Dutch village of Zundert slumbers,
he lies rocking in his wooden cradle, flame-haired,
a constellation of freckles sprinkling his cheeks.

His shining eyes change color—first blue, then green—
and dart after pink and yellow starlit shapes that twinkle
on the ceiling.

Vincent can't sleep . . .
Mother will fuss, Father will frown.
He might wake his little brother, Theo.

In half-light, his pencil drawings flicker
on the sloping beams of their attic room.

Carrying laced-up leather boots, he
tiptoes down narrow pine stairs, turns
the front latch, inching the door open to
a wild shimmer of midnight air.

Vincent can't sleep . . .
out, out, out he runs!
Flying through the garden—
marigold, geranium, blackberry, raspberry—

past the church with its tall steeple,
down rolling hills and sandy paths
meant for sheep.

He dives at last into the velvety,
violet heath, snuggles under a blanket
of sapphire sky, and looks up, up, up . . .
to
visit with
the stars.

Vincent can't sleep . . .

away at boarding schools in bigger towns. Zevenbergen. Tilburg.

Dull classes. Colorless teachers. Rainbowed memories of home.

While other students study, play, and laugh together,
Vincent draws, writes, and sighs alone.

He runs into the soothing darkness and is brought back to the
harsh light over and over again.

Vincent can't sleep . . .
though he's grown, working in gleaming cities—
The Hague, London, Paris.
    He stocks and sells paintings in Uncle's
fashionable galleries.

Excited. Bored. Eager.
Lazy. Explosive. Shy.
His many-colored moods
scare the customers—
and he's forced to go.

Vincent can't sleep . . .
wandering west in England, south in Belgium.
Teaching. Shopkeeping. Preaching.
His letters fill with roadside scenes—
peasants and thunderclouds inked along the way.

Now he calls himself an artist. The neighbors whisper. His family worries. Is Vincent lost?

He drifts—hundreds of miles in a tattered hat and cloak, framing haloed sunsets with charcoal-stained hands.

Vincent can't sleep . . .
and won't stop painting! He's found his light!
After scattered lessons from proper artists, he
takes off, canvas and paints strapped to his back.

Flashing brushstrokes capture country cottages at dusk,
city cafés at midnight, canvas after canvas like radiant
chapters in a book only Vincent can read.

He discovers that darkness is not plain black—
galaxies of color float on the night air.

Vincent can't sleep . . .
shut tight in a hospital. Told to rest as dark hills
wave past his window—first blue, then green.

He pictures a snuggling village, a flaming
cypress, a tall steeple pointing up, up, up . . .

Waits for morning when he's allowed to paint
and asks himself wild questions—

Does darkness have a texture?

Thick?

Thin?

Does it have a rhythm?

Quick?

Slow?

Is the night sky at rest? Or do eleven stars
pulse like a beating heart?

Then his painting stands finished,
a whirling, moonlit dream reflecting
the warm sun, bold and infinite, like
the wandering Milky Way, strange
and restless, like Vincent himself.

A sensitive boy.

A hidden genius.

A brilliant artist.

The one who knows best the many
colors of the night.

Shhh. Vincent's asleep.

Author's Note

Vincent van Gogh often couldn't sleep. From boyhood on, he was plagued with long bouts of insomnia in addition to many other symptoms of mental or physical illness. These kept him awake, wandering while others slept. Once around the age of nine or ten, he walked at night alone from his hometown of Zundert, in the Netherlands, and was found with torn clothes and muddy shoes in a town six miles away in the country of Belgium. As he grew older, he painted productively and lived much of his life in the hours between dusk and dawn.

Van Gogh's works include nearly 900 paintings, most completed in the years between 1881 and 1890. Vincent's art was influenced by the Barbizon school painter Jean-François Millet, as well as the Impressionists (Claude Monet, Camille Pissarro) and Post-Impressionists (Georges Seurat, Paul Signac, and Paul Gauguin). Few people during his lifetime appreciated Van Gogh's artistic talent; he was known more for his passionate energy and manic moodiness. Though he is now considered one of history's greatest artists, experts believe he sold fewer than five paintings in his lifetime. His dramatic paintings of sunflowers and irises use bright daytime colors, but many of his masterpieces are set in or around darkness, including the visionary oil painting *The Starry Night,* completed in 1889 while he was being treated at a hospital for those with mental illness in the town of Saint-Rémy-de-Provence in southern France.

The Starry Night combines reality with imagination and is widely considered one of the most important paintings in history. The scene is based partially on Van Gogh's eastern facing view from his bedroom window at the hospital. He could see a wheat field and the night sky over rolling hills, but he could not see a village from his room. The twinkling town in *The Starry Night* is composed from earlier sketches of Saint-Rémy, memories of his hometown of Zundert, or some imagined combination. He sketched many versions of this scene in pen and charcoal, but doctors did not allow him to paint in his room. *The Starry Night* was painted during the day between June 16 and 18, 1889, in the studio Vincent had set up downstairs.

The problem of painting "darkness that is still color" is one that Van Gogh wrestled with throughout his short, brilliant life. He solved it by loading his brushes with paint, then swirling or dashing strokes of complementary colors (reds with greens, purples with yellows, blues with oranges), which created luminous night scenes. His oil paintings demonstrate a masterful knowledge of composition, color mixing, and painting technique, such as impasto (painting thickly). Vincent's personality shines through his art—with each energetic brushstroke and wild color choice, he brings the night to life.

"At present, I absolutely want to paint a starry sky."
—Vincent van Gogh

The Starry Night, 1889. 73.7 x 92.1 cm.
The Museum of Modern Art,
New York City.

The Bedroom, 1889. 73.6 x 92.3 cm.
The Art Institute of Chicago.

Café-Terrace at Night (Place du forum in Arles),
1888. 80.7 cm x 65.3 cm.
Kröller-Müller Museum, Otterlo, Netherlands.

"It often seems to me that the night is much more alive and richly colored than the day."
—Vincent van Gogh

Sources

Art Institute of Chicago. Exhibit: *Van Gogh and Gauguin: The Studio of the South.* artic.edu/aic /exhibitions/vangogh/slide_intro.html.

Blumer, Dietrich. "The Illness of Vincent van Gogh." *American Journal of Psychiatry.* vol. 159. no. 4. pp. 519–526. April 2002.

Boime, Albert. "Van Gogh's *Starry Night:* A History of Matter and a Matter of History." *Arts Magazine.* vol. 59. no. 4. pp. 86–103. December 1984. albertboime.com/Articles/Dec1984.pdf.

Dirven, Ron. Director-conservator of Vincent van Gogh Huis, Zundert, Netherlands. Email communications 2/27/15.

Hulsker, Jan. *Vincent and Theo van Gogh: A Dual Biography.* Ann Arbor, MI: Fuller Publications, 1990.

Metropolitan Museum of Art: Vincent van Gogh. metmuseum.org/toah/hd/gogh/hd_gogh.htm.

Museum of Modern Art: The Collection. *The Starry Night.* moma.org/collection/object.php?object _id=79802.

Naifeh, Steven, and Gregory White Smith. *Van Gogh: The Life.* New York: Random House, 2011.

Pickvance, Ronald. *Van Gogh in Arles.* New York: MoMA/Harry N. Abrams, 1984.

Stein, Susan Alyson, ed. *Van Gogh: A Retrospective.* Fairfield, CT: Hugh Lauter Levin Associates, 1986.

Van Gogh Museum. vangoghmuseum.nl/en.

Van Heugten, Sjaar, Joachim Pissarro, and Chris Stolwijk. *Van Gogh and the Colors of the Night.* Amsterdam: Van Gogh Museum. New York: Museum of Modern Art, 2008.

Vincent van Gogh: The Letters. vangoghletters.org.

Wallace, Robert. *The World of Van Gogh, 1853–1890.* New York: Time-Life Books, 1969.

Welsh-Ovcharov, Bogomila, ed. *Van Gogh in Perspective.* New Jersey: Prentice-Hall, 1974.

Whitney, Charles A. "The Skies of Vincent van Gogh." *Art History.* vol. 9. no. 3. pp. 351–362. September 1986.

"If only you pay attention to it you will see that certain stars are lemon-yellow, others pink or a green, blue and forget-me-not brilliance. And . . . it is obvious that putting little white dots on the blue-black is not enough to paint a starry sky."

—Vincent van Gogh

For those who know darkness and still look for light.
—B.R.

For painters of all ages, who forge forward
in search of the light within.
—M.G.

ACKNOWLEDGMENTS

Many thanks to Gloria Groom, Chair of European Painting and Sculpture and
David and Mary Winton Green Curator, Art Institute of Chicago,
and Allison Perelman, Research Associate, Art Institute of Chicago,
for their careful reading and helpful comments on both text and art.

THIS IS A BORZOI BOOK PUBLISHED BY ALFRED A. KNOPF

Text copyright © 2017 by Barb Rosenstock
Jacket art and interior illustrations copyright © 2017 by Mary GrandPré
All rights reserved. Published in the United States by Alfred A. Knopf,
an imprint of Random House Children's Books, a division of Penguin Random House LLC, New York.

Knopf, Borzoi Books, and the colophon are registered trademarks of Penguin Random House LLC.

Visit us on the Web! randomhousekids.com

Educators and librarians, for a variety of teaching tools, visit us at RHTeachersLibrarians.com

Library of Congress Cataloging-in-Publication Data is available upon request.
ISBN 978-1-101-93710-5 (trade) — ISBN 978-1-101-93711-2 (lib. bdg.) — ISBN 978-1-101-93712-9 (ebook)

The text of this book is set in Horley Old Style with P22 Vincent.
Title hand-lettering by Leah Palmer Preiss.

The illustrations were created with acrylic, pen, and watercolor on board.

MANUFACTURED IN CHINA
October 2017
10 9

First Edition